For dear Jo

Many thanks for your
support.
All best wishes
from Anne
November 2nd 2011

The
Unmothering Class

I look forward to
reading your first
crime novel.

Anne Ryland

ARROWHEAD
PRESS

First published 2011 by
Arrowhead Press
70 Clifton Road, Darlington
Co. Durham, DL1 5DX
Tel: (01325) 260741

Typeset in 11 on 14pt Laurentian by
Arrowhead Press

Email: editor@arrowheadpress.co.uk
Website: http://www.arrowheadpress.co.uk

ISBN 978-1-904852-31-5

Printed and bound in Great Britain by
MPG Books Group, Bodmin and King's Lynn.

for David, as always

Acknowledgements

Thanks are due to the editors of the following where some of the poems in this book, or versions of them, first appeared:

Acknowledged Land; Acumen; Agenda; Artemis; Chapman; Envoi; Gategate (The Northern Writers' Centre, 2007); HerStoria; Images of Women (Arrowhead Press, 2006); The Interpreter's House; Kent and Sussex Poetry Society Poetry Folio; KJV: Old Text ~ New Poetry (Wivenbooks, 2011); Lit (Newcastle University, 2009); Long Poem Magazine; Magma; Mslexia; Northwords; Orbis; Other Poetry; The Red Wheelbarrow; Scintilla; Second Light Live; Second Light Newsletter; The SHOp; The Stinging Fly; Writers' Hub.

'The Twins' Heads' won first prize in the Kent and Sussex Poetry Competition (2009); 'Snegurochka' won joint second prize in the Second Light Competition (2007); 'For a Daughter' was runner-up in the Mslexia Competition (2007); and a longer version of 'The Secret Places of the Stairs' was Commended in the Ninth Scintilla Poetry Competition (2008).

I would like to thank all those who have so generously offered encouragement and guidance, particularly Moniza Alvi, Linda France and Pascale Petit.

I am most grateful to New Writing North for a Northern Promise Award, which assisted me in writing some of the earlier poems for this book.

My husband David and members of my family, especially Andrew, Jonathan and Martin Wright, and Moira Mitchell, have provided invaluable support. Dr Carol English has contributed her expertise in genetics. Hannah Kelson has been an understanding friend throughout.

Contents

* * *

Haunting My Daughter

* * *

The Ruin Withholds its Secrets

It disrupts the skyline –
my eye stumbles over juts and drops.

        This is no sanctuary.
        But there is so much room in a ruin,
        to tramp through a long hesitation.

A human in the ruins is less
than the whistle of a curlew across mudflats
or a single thrift swaying on the cliff.

        I love the silences of a ruin's story,
        the presence of murders and prayers.

I draw closer to touch
its scars and fractures –
immerse myself in brokenness.

        Where are the stairs that spiral
                beyond rooflessness?

When I wander among ruins, a longing grows in my throat.

        It has borne the ice, the salt-gnaw and the wars;
        it knows the triumph of being more
        than left over.

Such quiet defiance in a ruin,
it dares to be an outline.

Rebekah

"Two nations are in thy womb." Genesis

Already they were jostling within her –
one was a country of forest and moss,

bare feet pounding the earth.
Everything red-brown and sudden.

The other was open terrain, slippery
blue-grey. Water closing over,

no footprints left behind.
She composed her own map for each land.

Even the rain fell differently – it spattered
on trees or gashed against cliffs.

Through months she listened;
the two nations shared a language

yet the same word was a leaf
on one side, a pebble on the other.

She sensed a father-son and a mother-son.
How would she hold them together?

Could both be home or would one always
be in exile? She rested her palms

on their softness, their bones.
Twenty years of emptiness, and waiting –

all the love she'd stored would never
be enough to stave off a war.

Two Gardens
after Claire Goll

Last time we were here the path was dust.
Now rain has flooded it
from my eyes. What season is this?

Roses are washed wide open. Wherever
my glance falls, nettles sprout.
Everything drips, nothing is finished.

A horse is dragging itself through me,
the next world a crust in his eye.
Behind, a carriage with a couple inside.

One blackbird sings to another,
its song too sweet; I wipe it away.
My voice is rusted by the storms.

A stain runs down the evening.
You're so far ahead on the journey,
your hand is already a hundred years old,

and shrivelled, it slides out of mine.
We grow quiet as two gardens at night,
home to the beetles and the rain, the rain –

Iron Harvest, Flanders

When the earth that was churned
and rechurned into an old brown tide

is ploughed again, it surrenders
still more: bullets and shrapnel balls,

the yellow-crusted shells
farmers rest at the edge of their fields

for the army to dismantle or melt.
Mustard gas has bled

from caches below cemeteries.
Beware of collecting souvenirs.

A taste of rust in my mouth,
I hold my breath.

So much will never be understood:
who renewed the split-open shell case

by placing a figurine
of the Virgin Mary inside;

why the fusilier dug up two years ago
kept a Flemish Bible in heart-pocket;

how the soldier blasted
by an Iraqi mine could joke

there'll be no use
in his unit for a blind sniper.

The Siege Swallow
after Olga Berggolts

That first spring of the siege
after the bitterest winter
chewing leather, glue and paint,
Leningraders wore a badge

on their breast, a tin swallow
with a letter in its bill,
the words they daren't speak:
I am waiting for a letter.

The ice road had thawed;
they could only be reached
from the homeland by wings,
an aeroplane or a bird.

Messenger of spring, its long
tail streamers, its glossy blue-black,
the swallow was a promise
as they gathered chamomile.

And as they ate the tender grass
that feathered in the ruins,
and gnawed on pine branches,
sucking vitamins from needles,

they were compelled to scratch
letters below a kerosene lantern.
'Today we are without Volodia.
I am going on alone'.

Homing
after Olga Berggolts

The road home is as long as a war.
The track is scorched, each crater holds
a silent battle, a moaning wind, everywhere a sorrow
that all places border on nowhere.
Those lindens by my house are already stooping
towards me, the roof green, as if in welcome.
I once painted the door the carefree
red of my daughter's hair. Katya.
Remembering her is like staring into a fire
until the flames burn my eyes.
My rotting boots tug me on at the pace
of a gnarled pilgrim, or someone missing.
I have no use for maps; they make me more lost.
Every path of that town is written into me.
The rumour that it's been restored,
and not in a dream, has warmed it up. I smell it.
I'll linger on the fringe of the park, forgetting
the bodies frozen inside their coats,
still sitting on the benches at dawn.
Home. I shall touch the rope and the stone,
fold my arms around those who will never return.

Shell Shop

After running up and down years of stairs
and being renamed Mary by Ma'am,
I'm in uniform again, my trim black outline
lumped into grey dungarees.

Dust and smoke, day or night shift,
it's all the same without windows.
I try to colour myself –
an emerald turban, a ruby headscarf.

We all do. Look at us, scattered across
this old glove factory like so many parrots!
I don't know why our lips are juicy
with Auxiliary Red, as if we're longing

to kiss or be kissed.
Machines spit at us, hammers stutter.
We can't speak. Alone
with the innards of cylinders,

their silver bellies open,
their blood-oil staining our hands –
we have to scrub them till they're raw.
I've still got ten fingers,

treat my creations as gently
as a seamstress sewing dresses of silk.
Under a shower of white-hot shavings
I cut the case into shape, twine the coils

and always, at the last stage, a bolt
tightens in my neck, sparks dance behind my eyes.
Then it's just me and the bomb.
And the roar of a silence in which people go missing.

Woman Seated in the Underground
after Henry Moore

I'm on that platform where endless
empty trains rattle through without stopping.

Peering down a passage, I see her in a corner,
hands cradled in lap, shoulders sturdy as bridges.

She's a spiral of white scratches against the wall,
her face scribbled out almost to a skull.

Perhaps the layers preserved her from girders
falling in her ribcage. The war over, she never

unravelled, no longer knew how not to wait;
she remained in the shelter all these years, silent,

listening to yawns, to rumbles from the tunnels,
from the ink-washed night above, didn't

climb the stairs to the old watercolour morning.
I edge closer. She's a haze of dust and chalk.

Such a shy radiance – this stranger
might be the mother of London.

Snegurochka
after a Russian folk tale

I owned not a drop of blood.
The villagers tiptoed closer
in their hats and coats, shivered
at the pitch of my voice,
but there was hope in whiteness.
An old couple, long childless,
declared themselves my parents.
I melted their crusted faces
each time mine froze
into a different silvery smile.
A surprise that never ended,
I breathed lace over windows
and I frosted pastries
by singing glacial notes.
Some nights I draped myself
round the steeple
to fall asleep.

As the days grew milder
it was a burden
being their snow maiden;
a pain gnawed my ice-bones
so I scattered to flakes,
flurrying with the wind,
or let myself subside
into a drift by the road.
My parents dared not
embrace or kiss me –
I might thaw against
their skin, their lips,
their store of warmth.
I belonged to no one –
only to winter.

She-Who-Refuses-To-Choose-A-Husband
after an Inuit legend

A stranger dressed in finest bearskins
strode one morning over the crusted fringe
of our shore. He sang to me of his home
where hare and reindeer hung above the fire,
carved me a necklace from ivory,
each bead a herring with fins and scales.
I was weary of the name Uinigumasuittuq,
so when he promised to take me to the land
of the birds, I agreed to become his wife.

All through that icy journey by kayak
I dreamed of us nestled in feathers,
our lamps filled with oil. We arrived
at half-light. He stepped out, flung
the paddle and fanned his arms before me.
His nose sharpened into a hooked bill
with a spot as red as the sinking sun.
Silencing me with his one yellow eye,
he kraued that he was King of the Gulls,
ordered me to clamber on his back –
so black, without chinks, and the white
of his head and underside was flawless.
In a thunder of flapping we lifted up
and up. I calmed myself – his gliding
was like living a whole summer at once.

We settled on the cliff top in a dip
strewn with sticks, rotting fronds of kelp.
I saw no footprints or tracks, no friends.
From that time, no words came from him,
just owk-owk-owk, which even the slap
of wind couldn't drown. His call scraped
against me. All I could utter was Yes,
and No when he pecked my hair for tufts
to soften his bed. Swooping below
my surface, he knew how to pluck
my fears one by one: fish in his ocean.

He stayed away all day scavenging,
returned at night offering me a spine,
the stringy leg of a gull-chick in his beak.
Every hour I balanced in that place
was the bone-grey of winter, even the sea
so far beyond it turned to stone.
My cries froze in the air, my eyes hunted
the rock face till I swayed; a kind of flying.

One morning he left to follow a smell
as strong as a feast. The moment came.
I began to pick my way down, gripping
at ledges and cracks with claw-fingers.
A sudden gust whipped my flesh,
rumbled in my ears. Long wings soared
to white-glint speartips, and the sky darkened
into the bird who was my husband.

The House-tree

At first they were the masters of their new home,
restoring it with an army of roaring machines,
but soon they complained of irritation
in their lungs, of restlessness in the floorboards.
Ceilings were growing taller than ladders.

One morning they found the piano clinging
to the eaves by its legs, black plunging on white.
They tried to coax it down. It dropped
its keys like dead fingers. Tunes rained on them,
soot and dust notes left floaters in their ears.

The husband shattered a window for air
and crystal-grit splintered his wife's skin.
Her voice flew out of the jagged holes.
The earth was too far below for them to jump.
Now the house was sprouting roots like an elm

worming a thousand-year home in the soil.
They tried drawing up water through its xylem cells.
It was too slow. It was too quiet.
Acid sap rose in the woman's throat;
such thirst for sunlight pouring through the door.
But already they were unknown at this address.

Moving In to Gwen John's Room
after 'A Corner of the Artist's Room in Paris'

Chair, table, window.
The room of a life pared down
to its roots and juices,
where work is always beginning
and rest waits under the eaves.
That firm old bed in the corner
will do me no harm.
I arrive without clutter, and learn
the bliss of clearance.
Visitors will be letters
and my own footsteps on the stair.
I belong on the top floor,
a quilt of roofs spread before me.
I keep running my eye
up and down the sloped ceiling.
The chalky shades of ochre
and lemon could almost
be rubbed away. I let them stay.
Everything is a suggestion:
an indigo velvet coat
draped on the chair, or a dusty cloth
tossed over it? And this lace curtain –
or is it a spillage of sun?
A place where I can leave a book
open, come home to the breeze
reading the pages through my window.
This wicker chair for company,
the web of its diamonds.

The Star Swallower

At first it had been enough
to wander in her garden of stars, learning the lesson
   of acceptance. *Women*
who keep reaching for the highest shelf will tumble
   warned her mother.
Scaremongers claimed those who numbered stars
   would be struck dead.
But she let herself be charmed by the dreamkeeper:
   if she counted ninety-nine
stars on nine nights in a row, her wish would
   be granted. Tilting her head,
she counted with her breath, jaw unclasped.
   Each night she swept
the ceiling of the world; each star a thousand
   million years, fresh-minted.
Until the ninth night – a star, adrift and sinking,
   flitted between her lips.
She tried to spit it out but it was frozen – needles
   barbed her tongue –
and when she tried to scream, ice crystals flew out
   in a silent song. Too late.
The star had melted against the roof of her mouth.
   It was fizzing-running
down her throat and would spark every word
   she'd never spoken.
It would flood the tidy cupboards of her body.
   She would be silvered in.

Midsummer Night, Berwick

The half-hearted darkness at eleven,
a sliver of night that is and is not a night.

I run my mind over the land, the surprises
of its plunging, coves with no footprints.

So many thresholds. Sea and stone
left words and prayers behind long ago.

Castles appear closer than they really are,
signs are hazy – *To the North* –

yet we follow, transhumant creatures
always climbing to remoter pastures.

Sometimes I wish I rose at dawn
to bake bread or deliver letters in the mist

but summer is just an interlude here
like loganberries or happiness.

How much has been postponed

So far I have not followed this river to its source
or explored the undertow of my life
on a northern border. I still haven't climbed
the newel staircase of the queenliest castle
to watch over dawn from the bartizan.
I excused myself from the post of ruinkeeper.
I've never written a letter to winter
or received its answer in the ice; neither
have I unpacked all the books in the attic,
shuffled through their crusty pages
in case a message flutters out. I have deferred
learning Russian though I keep roaming Siberia
in a shaman's coat, and why do I remember
words like *Vergangenheitsbewältigung*
when I've failed to master Let Go?
So far I have not rinsed my hands in a lavabo,
observed how much there is to be washed away,
then gathered the strength to mend wounds
within those I love, within my empty room.

Northern Answer Lady

The first questions to trickle in
were simple: *Where is Peep O' Sea?*

Soon the teasers
were rolling towards her –
What is the name of the fifth season
when summer's passed but autumn's dawdling?

Alone as a lighthouse keeper above the rocks
she started falling
into a well of questions.
The don't-knows gnawed her sleep.

Are northerners predictable?
She tried to calm the enquirers who demanded
answers clear and sharp as glass

but found herself tied up in knots
as if she'd been struck by the old wind-witch.

The north was roaming about, spilling
over its borders. Kings had failed to pin it down.
Why are there so many norths?
Some had even flitted over the top of maps.

The northern winter caught her out,
already on her shoulder.
She was floating
through an icy underworld, asking
Where is the north? Is it outside – or inside?

I told no one

According to selkie legend, the children left behind by a seal woman on her return to the ocean, may, unwittingly or otherwise, have assisted their mother's escape.

I was the youngest, with webbed hands and feet.
I followed her when she wandered
down the crumbly steps dug into the cliff.
She'd stare out till the skerries appeared at low tide,
or into the fog bank – for hours.
She didn't sing any more; she barked,
kept sending me down to the ebb for whelks.

One afternoon I gashed my foot on a flint.
Rubbing goose grease over my soles,
she promised to sew me a pair of slippers
soft as fleece. *I'm rummlin' fur the bonnie skin,*
she said, flichtering about as if she'd hidden it
somewhere in the cottage. *Mam,* I babbled,
I ken whar it is! and pointed up the chimney –
I'd spied my faither groping about there
while everyone else was asleep, he thought.
Yes, it was me. I witnessed the fur pour
over my mam, her shoulders, her arms.
That rainbow-of-grey sealskin coat, falling
to her ankles. Her almost greedy snort.
Immersing her neck in the collar, she whispered
O bairn, dinnae tell. I patted her cream chest,
didn't nestle my face or I might never have come out.
With sticks, we poked the coat back into its nook.

Next morning she scaulded *It's time you were gaun*
tae raik the clift fur gulls' eggs. Mind and dae it!
I almost choked on the bannock she'd baked;
dragged home an empty basket. I was feart.
A message on my pillow: swirls and scratches.
Half-limping, I ran down the cliff steps to the shore,
tracked my mam across the damp sand,
until her footprints petered out. A silent gap.
Beyond that, what I knew were flipper strokes,
shy-smiling lips, and the grooves carved by her belly
as she'd flopped away. I offered her the songs
she'd washed over me – *I heard a mither*
ba-ing her bairn ... The waves were stronger,
the wind slapping me like the sweeps of a tail.

My faither declared Mam missing at sea –
an accident on the cliff or by the rip tide.
The village elders blethered it was for the best;
she would've been a disturbance in the graveyard.
I found a pair of pearl-grey slippers below my bed.
I wasn't a girl any more. But I wasn't a seal.
My mother never led me down the stairs
to her underwater world. Sometimes I basked
on the haul-outs, the rocks warming my back.
Or I listened to the howls from the cove
where human boots could not go.

Seal Song

Her mouth opens wide and she calls –
longer than a moan, an unbroken note
that floats for thirteen seconds
and settles in the wind. The ocean stills.
When the haar rolls in
she will warn lost fishermen of rocks.
Her underwater eyes spill into mine.
She might be hundreds of years old,
her scarred head restoring itself on the waves.
Silver shades to cream on her belly.
With claws elegant as fingernails
she strokes herself,
then rests both flippers; hands remembering.
Her voice startles the roots of my hair
as if I have swum in it.
Does she still turn to hush
her ghost-pup in its cradle of oarweed?
I would be capturing fish with my hands
if I tried to write the sorrow of her song –
it holds blue light from the ocean floor,
all the shades of white in her child's lanugo.

* * *

Haunting My Daughter

Note to Haunting My Daughter

The poems in the sequence are written in the imagined voices of my female ancestors. The surname Wright, my maiden name, was often a source of frustration in my family history research, yet also ultimately liberating; the dearth of information left me free to invent. The poems are my versions of my ancestors' lives but bear, I hope, an emotional truth.

It is clear that most of 'my women' were barely literate. Furthermore, women's occupations were usually considered not worth recording on census returns or birth, marriage and death certificates, although working class women invariably toiled throughout their lives to ensure the survival of their families. These women had neither a spoken nor a written voice; I wanted to redress this.

Patterns emerged, with some women following in their mother's footsteps while others resolved, it seemed, to carve their own path. More tantalizing still were the discrepancies, the silences and the absences, which gradually began to tell their own stories. Although General Registration was introduced in England in 1837, such factors as evasion tactics, clerical errors and variant spellings of names resulted in people slipping through the official net. Equally, those who apparently disappeared may well have died lonely, anonymous deaths in the workhouse, or on the streets.

I am indebted to a number of sources for my research, most notably to 'Victorian Women' by Joan Perkin (John Murray, 1993), 'Women in England 1760 – 1914' by Susie Steinbach (Phoenix, 2004) and 'My Ancestor was an Agricultural Labourer' by Ian Waller (Society of Genealogists, 2007).

My grandmother and great-grandmother, Annie Wright and Mary Wright, were 'brought alive' for me by my aunt. Above all I would like to thank my cousin, Martin Wright, for locating a copy of a crucial document bearing the names and some key dates of all ten siblings of our great-grandfather, Charles Wright.

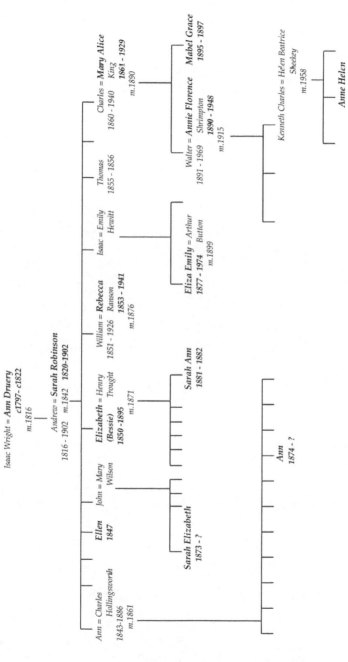

Isaac Wright = **Ann Druery**
c1797- c1822
m.1816

Andrew = **Sarah Robinson**
1816 - 1902 m.1842 **1820-1902**

Ann = Charles
Hollingsworth
1843-1886
m.1861

Ellen
1847

John = Mary
Wilson

Elizabeth = Henry
(Bessie) Trought
1850 -1895
m.1871

William = **Rebecca**
1851 - 1926 Ranson
1853 - 1941
m.1876

Isaac = Emily
Hewitt

Thomas
1855 - 1856

Charles = **Mary Alice**
1860 - 1940 King
1861 - 1929
m.1890

Mabel Grace
1895 - 1897

Walter = **Annie Florence**
1891 - 1969 Shrimpton
1890 - 1948
m.1915

Kenneth Charles = Helen Beatrice
Sheekey
m.1958

Anne Helen

Sarah Elizabeth
1873 - ?

Sarah Ann
1881 - 1882

Ann
1874 - ?

Eliza Emily = Arthur
1877 - 1974 Button
m.1899

The Wright Family

Names of those who are the subject of poems appear in bold

25

Baptising One Day, Burying the Next

Haunted by her mother –
matted and leathered, supping burnt crust tea –
still the cordwainer's daughter marries the prentice,
hammers herself into the cordwainer's wife.

So there he was, just nineteen – Isaac, a boot-jack
between his knees, mouth crammed with sprigs,
spitting them out one by one, like curses.
Shoes hanging from shop walls and ceiling,

the midnight tapping never stopped.
Picture me, already bark-tanned and tallowed,
spiking holes with my awl, stitching tongues to uppers.
Loud, hard, cold.

Until Andrew, my firstborn.
My softest work, made in a place I didn't know,
he was satin on my skin.
                    But then I left a son
in every parish. Baptising one day, burying the next.

I staggered on, Andrew tugging at my skirt.
My other sons were blue-grey knots.
Sewing shrouds – the linen blackened in my hands.
I ran in white kid slippers, vanished

into this name: mine, yours.

Ann Wright
c1797-c1822

Stone-picking in a Mist

There were more of my children now on the other side than this.
I'd always cradled soft, wriggling bodies
awkwardly as white coffins,
but for each one my back cracked
picking turnips and twitch, and my hands bled.

I was locked in a smoke-thick room,
baking bread for the eleven mouths, a panic of beaks.
The book I couldn't read
taunted me – *her candle goeth not out at night ...*

Wandering round the pond where Thomas gossiped
with the ducks and drowned.
Out on the land harrowing,
I'd left Ann, my eldest, minding him.
My ninth child, only a year and a half,
stout as a little bailiff.
There he was on his belly, arms opened in welcome.
I collapsed next to him panting,
                              as if giving birth once more.

Planting in the fields,
too bright by far in a red scarf. Still bleeding.
I should've carried her on my back,
rested her below a hedge.
The dearest of my three girls.
Tired after five days of life, she went, sudden. Ellen.
I did not need God to scold me that I lost my daughter
                              because of the potatoes.

For a while I was a girl again, roaming in a silvery mist
like the one over meadows at dawn,
stone-picking with my small rake,
or shouting and running about
in my bright blue smock to scare off the birds.

Who was that crabby old man – my father? Or my husband?
He shooed me into a cottage, said it was my home.
I turned my head to the wall and moaned.

A village whisper –
'softening of the brain'.

Sarah Wright
1820-1902

A Splinter

Before I was here
I was gone.
I was the silence

after my mother's scream
but my eyes were alive,
cornflower blue.

I was forever
the splinter
under her skin,

mourned by her alone –
I was a raindrop,
that's all,

never grew into Ellen,
into more or less
than anyone hoped for.

What did I miss?
A damp-warped cottage,
the plait school,

down the aisle
with a ploughman,
laughing the harvest dance:

not so much. Enough.
Don't pass me by –
I still have breath.

Ellen Wright
born 1847, died aged 5 days

30

Thrashing the Holy Linens

1   When Henry Trought turned up, I was twenty and unwed,
ripe enough to throw off the names Elizabeth and Betsy.
His blue uniform had a gold braid. Henry, a station porter.
No mud-caked boots. Too swift and smooth for a plough
he was, promised to get me up and moving, on
the rails, away from the farm, Ma and Pa, all the Wrights.

After our Sunday strolls, and me dawdling on his platform,
it was time for a wedding. No fuss. All through the service
I held my thumb free when Henry clasped my hand,
to warn him he'd never raise his hand to me.
Besides, I had sturdy arms from the fields, hacking swedes.
In the marriage register I signed myself as Bessey.
(The trouble I had spelling it out.)

How was I to guess I'd ride on a train just once?
Northwards to his home town, Hull. To Rose Terrace –
not a petal in sight – the same brown-damp rooms as before,
except with docks and drunks, the fish-and-piss stink.
My husband whistled off in his cap to find work.
I already knew we'd be tossed up and down in the world.

2   In six years we built a staircase of boys!
Five bellies to fill, five grubby faces, but they were ours.
Like their father, they obeyed. (My hands were rough.)
On Sundays I cooked bacon scraps or ox cheek in a pot.
By Thursday it was bread and treacle. I sometimes
went without. We kept off poor relief, I saw to that,

set myself up as a laundress. It was as backbreaking
as thistle picking or forking out witch grass – but indoors.
I took in washing from the vicarage. On Blue Monday
I'd be thrashing the holy linens with the dolly,
rubbing soap and soda through, dissolving the blue dye
so they'd not turn yellow. Wash and rinse twice, boil, rinse –

the rector's vestments rained from our ceiling all week.
His sermons never seeped into me: far too black and white.
Neighbours and idlers used to sneer *Sweaty Bessie!*
Not in my hearing though. They wouldn't dare.
That steam kept me and my sons clean on the inside.
I believed, then, we could survive without prayers.

3   Last born, first gone. Sarah Ann. Our only daughter.
I bestowed on her the old names from my mother,
my grandmother. She bloomed ten months, no years,
but never saw autumn – she was my orchard, more
than all the flushed reds and dark golds, the aroma
of apples and pears. One word on paper: diarrhoea.

4   No surprise when the typhoid arrived. A bitter winter
didn't stamp it out. My boys weren't sickly chaps,
just listless. 'Influenza,' I thought. Fresh air
was ordered by the doctor – as if I could catch it in a sack!
My sons were writhing with the sweats. Swollen bellies,
pink spots clustering on their chests. The long sleep,

not yet death. I sponged their brows, whispering,
wishing. Oh, the vigil! Forced to sit still, I witnessed
the mould growing, walls dripping their brown tears.
Freddie and George were taken from us, two days apart.
It was the smell of Hull that killed them. I went missing
in all that quiet.

5   The Troughts were no longer the right shape: three gaps.
Scabs to pick at. Heart-rot. Henry drank and drank.
As a girl on the farm I could drive the crabbiest bullocks
out to the field – they listened to me. Now, when he
blundered in at dawn, I'd slump my face in the pillow.

One November after midnight, as Henry was overseeing
the cargo of the SS Urbino, he slipped, and fell
into the river. Gasps and shrieks. A light was lowered
over the edge of Alexandra Dock – only his hat afloat.
It was hours before the grappling irons dragged him out.

Dr Redhead pronounced his life extinct,
so our Harry read to me from the Hull Daily Mail.
Despite the ale, Henry hadn't been a bad soul, no fists.
I was both heavy and empty. Head of the family,
three sons left. How to keep us all out of the workhouse?

6   I took in another docker. Rumours spread he was more
than a boarder. Mr Turner was a broad shoulder
to shore me up a while. He paid for his extras, his laundry.
                                  Love? No, never.

All along the typhoid was in hiding. Harry, my pride,
my eldest, a school teacher. He died. There was no word
for a mother who'd lost her strongest son. He'd towered
                                above his father.

A washing dolly was churning inside me, rose-spots
were gathering on my breast. When they lifted me at last
into the sanatorium, I sighed at the taste of a delicious mist.
                                I smiled.

Bessie Trought
1850-1895

Rowing Towards Autumn

All summer I opened at dawn, rowing
    towards autumn with my arms and lungs.

I lifted a foot, my first step – wobbly legs.
    I was burbling when the poison seeped in.

My belly screamed and my throat burnt.
    Mama was soft, and tough. She stormed

against the Lord, the oozing brown walls,
    the gnawing. No, it wasn't her fault.

Flies danced on me, I slid behind my eyes.
    Oh, this time I never waved her goodbye.

She washed and dressed me, not a shroud,
    but a white nightgown edged with lace,

so clean I was almost reborn. I was pulsed
    away in a boat, passing the wharf, nudged

along the Humber and out into the fresh
    sea, the salt-and-sparkle. I heard the sigh

of *Sarah   Sarah   Sarah* over the water –
    was it Mama calling, adrift on the shore?

Sarah Ann Trought
1881-1882

Spinning Cobwebs

1   There was nothing special about me,
just a housemaid, not creamy-skinned.
Two cottages away, a stocky boy lodger
sat outside each evening dubbining his boots.

A farm labourer, he always nodded hello.
Not one for the girls, though, William Wright –
maybe that's why he chose me.
Didn't even tempt me up the ladder

into the tickly hayloft for the proving.
Him one of eleven, me one of five –
I could already see us in a crowd of little faces.
A good match. A quiet winter wedding.

2   I tried everything.
The pennyroyal and the dock. Not once
did I look at the full moon through glass.
Kind (or was it poor?) Auntie Becky,

I was a *There, there* and a chunk of bread.
I sewed a rag doll for every niece,
offered her a bed when she became a spare
daughter, squashed out of her home,

while I dragged along the babies we couldn't have,
but I never had to worry
about them or bury them in white boxes
with lily-of-the-valley sprinkled on top.

Each cottage we lived in I kept cleaner than the last.
I stayed regular with church.
It was God's will, the parson smiled,
and I said *Yes*. My heart said *Why?*

3   William set off at dawn for his threshing machine –
sweet-talked it like it was his horse.
True, he spoke more to it than to his wife
but he came back to me every night.

I stayed home for the outwork.
Lace. Worse than spinning cobwebs.
Twelve hours a day bent over the pillow:
pricking the patterns, battling with bobbins.

The scrubbing, scrubbing of hands
sucked the colour out of me.
My eyes throbbed. Slowly the world lost
its sharp edges. Yet the evenings grew soft.

I'd sit, a book on my lap, fancying I could read,
or make up stories in my head.

4   The only children I was granted who were not
borrowed, were withered –
my mother- and father-in-law.
I calmed their babbling, mopped their brows.

Then after fifty years together, William too.
Pneumonia in June. He still didn't let go
of his secrets. I was left alone with the words
of the stone. 'Though lost to sight, to memory dear.'

5   Afterwards I held myself tall.
People told me I had a sparkle.
I lived on and on, was photographed
in my dark blue jersey-knit suit,

an old woman with new spectacles.
I stand out from among the dead.

Rebecca Wright
1853-1941

Red-ochreing Doorsteps

She swigged cold rue tea and hot gin.
    No use, though. Even the kick of his boot
        didn't dislodge me. I was the ninth

too many. She was rag-patched and blue-grey –
    still I clung to her like sweat, obeyed her.
        Whenever she wiped me off

I stayed silent – no need for opiates.
    But she often nibbled dry bread
        so I'd have a dab of butter on mine.

The smallest, often made to eat under the table,
    I felt myself slipping through cracks.
        I was out all day, red-ochreing doorsteps.

Once Pa came back, our step was treacherous.
    That winter Ma was draining away.
        He warned me I'd soon be an orphan.

Delivered me to the workhouse.
    Just a while, he said, to ease the burden.
        I disappeared, or maybe was hidden

behind the whitewashed glass
    of the classroom, among striped aprons,
        cropped hair and too many prayers.

I broke out into the cough-and-shivers.
  Fever – Ma's gift. I clawed the walls
    for her till God took me to the paupers'

corner. I wouldn't, won't, be quiet any more.
  You worry about me? Worry
    is not far from love.

Ann Hollingsworth
1875-?

Running Along the Furrows of Shirts

For years I was their glory, the only child.
Until two brothers arrived. I lost my foothold.

Scraping mud off boots and darning socks,
I was no more than a maid-of-all-work

to Charles and Thomas. Their muscles and bones
hardened in the fields, their eyes dulled to stones,

while I was stored indoors
like milk in the ewer, turning sour.

Plain (no one said 'ugly') but respectable,
I wouldn't shackle myself to a bull

of a chap like Alf Brunt, who tried to grab
my leg for a bundling. I was waiting for my hand

to be clasped, for the banns, the vows.
Little chance. Every day, trapped for fourteen hours

in one room. Slop work – call it what you want –
no daughter was allowed to say *I won't*.

Such ardent running along the furrows of shirts,
but I'd never listened to a man's heart

or sniffed his skin. My machine owned
me. With Ma and Pa shrinking to husks, I sewed

on and on till the whiteness was blinding,
and all I saw was me winding

down to stitching shrouds to earn another shilling.
I longed for a new beginning, for spring,

set forth on a mosaic quilt, a double.
Roaming in primroses and violets, I was hopeful,

thought I could patch myself a marriage.
Below my bed, an ending, a mildewing package.

I was musty, past thirty. My brothers were gruff.
The worry of whether they'd offer me a roof

or whether I'd be a distressed seamstress,
left in the workhouse. Or worse.

Sarah Elizabeth Wright
1873-?

Mending Ends on the Underside

I'd seen enough of girls going afield –
from dawn till dusk following
the reaper, backs stooping, with a child

left screaming in a bundle under a tree.
And then in winter, their arms and legs growing
skinnier, bluer. That would never be me.

I married a man whose machines
were indoors. Arthur set about removing
me from the farm, somewhere warmer, cleaner

he promised, yet soon as we'd stepped off the train
in Manchester I gasped for breath, choking
on the fog that was smoke. I paled,

let the city swallow me. Soon I was off to the mill.
The filth, the din, the bellowing
of those weaver lasses – the stories I could tell –

but they showed me the tricks, how to suck weft
through the hole in the shuttle. Cotton was snowing
down my throat into my chest,

clung to my lungs. Coughed home. No child. Was
I sorry? In nightmares I still heard his moaning,
the little boy who sipped from the big kettle. The blaze

of his eyes when boiling water baptised him in a tide –
my *No No No* echoing.
I was nine, minding him. No one blamed me. I did.

My fingers tingled. I withdrew to a corner. Years
started whirring. Buttoning (ha!) and gloving,
hemming handkerchiefs. Mopping women's tears,

I was forever 'helping out'.
Aunts, nieces, neighbours, strangers. There was nothing
I didn't know about vigils and funerals. Me, devout?

No, I was an invisible mender of ends
on the underside, a stem stitch flowing
through lives. Arthur called it the fine industry of hands.

I called it 'keeper of guilt and secrets'.
Even past ninety I was flowering
my grey life with violet knots.

Eliza Emily Button
1877-1974

Haunting my Daughter

1   I was an old bride, nearly thirty. Love wasn't
      my dream. Rather, belonging to him, my own parlour.
        Why Charles with his tight-curled hair, almost roguish?

He'd crossed oceans – he might well have left
   little Wrights in other ports.
      I was At Home, a civil servant's daughter. Unspoilt.

My husband understood machines –
   a member of The Amalgamated Society of Engineers –
      no diagrams, though, for the workings of his wife.

I never saw the farm, or his mother and father,
   or heard the names of the two brothers and three sisters
      who'd died. The past. A country he didn't visit.

The past. My home. From Dublin to London –
   West Ham, East Ham, Ilford – it made no difference.
      I belonged nowhere. A *Good Morning* set me apart.

My voice was a fast river, and if it flooded
   I saw cockneys thinking *blarney* or *brood.*
      The black rock always inside me.

2   Walter was prompt, nine months after the wedding.
All frowns and bones, he was already far too old.
He grew longer and stronger

but no younger. A boy who stored his thoughts
in caskets, labelled. I observed him,
that slanting right eye, for signs of what – a fracture?

*

Our second child – she was everything I'd yearned for.
By her first birthday, Mabel was *Mama*-ing
and laughing with me.

    It was just a tickle in her throat.
    The cough growled down to her chest,
    she started barking, her back arched –
    the whoop almost split her open.
    I gave her syrup of squills, laudanum drops.
    The doctor told me *Bundle her up,*
    take her for a ride on top of the omnibus.
    A bit of air to sweep her out, no need to fret.
    We came home blackened with soot.
    On and on, a lullaby bleeding through the nights,
    her hacking, me hushing,
                    but I could not give her my breath.

Her coffin was too white for the dark parlour.
A candle burning both ends, the mirror
turned to the wall.

3   A year rusting in black crêpe,
        then a dress of black wool. I was caught
        in half-mourning, grey.

           Each night I waited for Charles to snore,
              or I'd push him off as soon as he was near
                it. I dried up. A fissure ran through me.

*

I started filling the parlour as if it were my heart.
A whatnot to display porcelain and ornaments,
the mantelpiece lined with glass lustre drops.
Everything draped – the lamps, the slow clock,
the mirror, the piano. Embroidered antimacassars,
memorial samplers: 'When the Lord thought it best,
He took me to a place of rest.' Walter stayed out.
The room made his eyes ache, Charles said.
I placed the chairs in a conversational manner.

*

A home circle, curtains   drawn, walls dissolved
my hands trembling   I listened for a sigh
the spirit trumpet to my ear   coals creaked
a glow from beyond   but she did not come
she never left a message   to comfort me –
I could not stop   haunting my daughter.

4   Everyone was retreating. Charles
          away on the distilleries. Even Walter,
              off to the war, after he'd married Annie,

a shadowy soul. Thankful to be my lodger,
      she read me snippets of his letters: 'It is not quiet
         here at the moment.' The roar of howitzers

gave my son 'gunner's ears', silenced
      the few words he'd ever had. I did miss him,
         wondered if he let *her* in to his secrets.

                    *

My eyes were gritty and bloodshot.
      I saw haloes. The doctor brushed me off:
         low spirits and excessive work in the brain.

I scurried home through the city
      with its blackened bricks and smutted faces.
         Charles turned on his charm –

gained me entrance to Moorfields, no less.
      The new doctors traced a grey-green haze
         in my pupils: glaucoma. I retired to the twilight.

5   My great-granddaughter, what we share
is a longing to converse with ghosts.
Leaning towards the dark, don't we almost sparkle?

Mary Alice Wright
1861-1929

Jolting the Well-sprung Wolseley

Why did they call me *Mabel?* I should've been a Cicely.
My father left the farms to be a millwright –
I could've broken out too, in a midnight
blue skirt twelve inches off the ground, a stocking-flash on risky

rides by bicycle. I might've boarded the trams as a clippie.
Picture me in a cobalt jacket with a riot
of brass buttons, punching tickets,
flying up and down the open staircase, all racy and chirrupy.

I would've gone to France, jolting the well-sprung Wolseley,
cajoling the engine to life under fire,
swabbing burns and mustard-tears.
But pertussis, the whoop, tombstoned me as Mama's ghostly

little darling. Don't file me with our upright family.
Grant me the bliss of over-
taking, or coupling with a lover,
my service boots and corset unlaced – the chance to be flighty.

Mabel Grace Wright
1895-1897

Touching a Sailor's Collar

1   In Aunt's house, I was a girl standing on a stool:
scraping and scrubbing, boiling.
My companions, the wringer and the mangle,
the coal scuttle – below the wafts of gossip.

To keep a bed and a roof, I had to be small.
No trooping the streets with banners,
no purple and green, no corsets and curlers.
No Vitaloids, no 'hysteria', no passing fancies,

until the tall, unsmiling man next door
asked me for a Sunday stroll by the river.
All Friday night, I tacked and hummed a skirt,
five inches off the ground, the shade of charcoal.

I was a mystery – he wouldn't let go. Or was it pity?

*

I had nimble wrists, and busy hands
older than the rest of me. Secretly
I longed to be a letter sorter,
to wander in blue ink, in copperplate,

crisp, clean paper between my fingertips,
no mistress except the General Post Office.
Me – a tiny link in the great chain
of the nation's mail. Each letter, a story.

My dream blotted out by the entrance test fee.

2   I was proud to be marrying a shipping clerk,
now Royal Garrison Artillery. He'd never laugh
even in peacetime, I knew, and chose not to mind.
West Ham Register Office, three guests. So quiet,

I swear we heard the roar of the guns over there.
I wore a hobble skirt as dark as ink,
a white blouse I'd whirred on my Singer
with lace collar and cuffs, an opal locket.

The hairy fabric of Walter's tunic
brushed my fingers – I tried not to think
of the field dressing sewn into his inner pocket.
The Front pounding nearer, like a heartbeat.

He was gone before I could grow into his wife.

*

I lodged with Charles and Mary, his parents.
Her torrent of chatter, her hair piled up,
haughty. 'Tea parties' in the dark parlour –
russet bows, glass domes over ornaments –

where she invited her favourite guests,
the dead. The mother from Dublin; the angel
daughter Mabel. A spirit trumpet to her ear,
my mother-in-law cooed *Darling, are you there?*

She drifted back with 'requests'. *Would you mind – ?*
I did mind her half-drawn eyes. We, the living,
were too low down for her. Evenings dragged
with migraines, a vinegar rag on my brow. I left.

53

*

In the factory behind the cathedral,
my machine clacked like a train. I treadled
through the not-knowing years – up and down
the pleats and tucks, in and out lattices.

Choosing mother-of-pearl buttons for a blouse,
I grew small things into jewels,
admiring their lustre as I nibbled a sandwich
in the shade of St Paul's. Not inside. No prayers.

Walter's latest letter, tucked in my pocket.
'Rain all day, trenches sloshy. I am all right.'
Whenever I spotted a sailor at the docks,
I'd run to touch his collar for luck.

I could manage without God, thank you.

3   My stern husband
strode down the road in his bowler hat.
Neighbours smirked: *Oo the 'ell does 'e fink 'e is?*
At night he fretted over ranks of figures. His terror of mistakes.

My raw sons –
I love-spun them bit by bit.
A month in bed with phlebitis, my legs under a cage.
I was past forty, a half-pint of a woman with a rattling chest,

but I advanced
to the front line. The twins bellowed
at a wedding in church, trembled together at school.
They grew stronger, squabbled, pretended to be each other.

4   Darkness fell once more, and settled.
I had so many lives to look after.
'Mothers: send them out of London!' I couldn't.
The boys had to stay with me

I'd not pin labels on them, like parcels, for Wales.
How to fatten them on Siege Cake,
keep the rascals clean with a lick and a promise.
The siren would go and I'd catch them up a tree!

Blackout nights of shadows, the cat warming my toes.
I stitched a butter muslin into a blouse,
dreamed cups of strong, sweet tea.
Outside, all those ghosts groping
                              along the road home.

*

I'd never nestled in Walter's arms but he lifted me,
as I coughed and wheezed, into the concrete shelter.
Then off he'd go to perch all night on a roof, on firewatch.
A wet sack over the door. We clutched our masks.

Their planes droning over to the gasworks –
this war choked me, the smoke and the panic.
Soft crumps. A bomb dropping close – the sound of silk
ripping, or a jagged fingernail snagging on the sky.

Our home crushed. Grey shapes in the rubble. That hush.

*

A bomber's moon. The siren swooping to a howl.
Bone-weary. Bournvita for 'peacetime sleep'. My pillow.
My sons, down the shelter. The sky spread a blood-red glow.
Dust in my lungs. My first prayer. Or last. For breath. For dawn.

5   Never spoken of. I didn't know,
but it seeped into me as I grew,
like damp. A greyish stain –
baseborn, by-slip, misbegotten.

I learned to sew invisible stitches,
play the piano as softly as an apology.
I signed my name in tiny letters
with the same swirl to the *A* as yours.

My granddaughter, I missed you
by years, and now you miss me.
Please don't say that *b-* word.
This is where you come from.

*

From me you receive
twig ankles and wrists,
the small, neat script,
an eye for the mis-stitch.

Annie Florence Wright
1890-1948

* * *

'I'm sorry to trouble you, but'

Once, near the end, our heads resting on her pillow,
she said, *I'm worried about troubling the vicar.*

By then she was having to bother the young doctor,
a swirl of petal-coloured nurses and carers,

her crumbling husband, her three children
who'd travelled hundreds of miles, to listen

as she fretted about buying their school shoes
and telling them the story of the birds and the bees.

Did she regret disturbing the undertakers so early,
long before dawn, on that sultry morning in July?

She could hardly avoid imposing on the embalmer,
the pall-bearers who carried the five stone of her,

the mourners who gathered in an unexpected throng
like blackbirds – and weren't sure how to sing,

the man playing the organ so quietly she could leave
discreetly, the lily arranger and the floor sweeper.

Finally, she was, after all, obliged to trouble the new
vicar, who'd only seen her through our eyes;

he proclaimed Helen Wright 'a gifted mother'.
I imagined her face flushing at this honour –

but no, by now she'd be mustering her courage,
the appropriate words for one last apology.

'Don't worry about your new school'
my mother's last words

The school had twenty storeys. I was forty, and lost,
jostled along stone corridors by a brutal draught.
Climbing the open spiral staircase was the first test –

I wobbled. The uniform was a woolly armour.
My satchel dragged me; the textbooks I had to bear
full of dank questions. I knew none of the answers.

In lessons I feared the restless footsteps on the floor
above; the invisible headmaster timetabling who
would cop the red spot or win the silver star

next. Every minute I was dreading his bell would go.
The nurse doled out lint to the overwrought,
lozenges for a permanent tear in my left eye.

The teacher thought I was still Anne Wright,
scratched a lesson for me on her blackboard:
my surname from *wyrcan*, to work. I wrote

myself out and away into foggy fields not recorded
in my trusty OED, flirted with thaumatology,
the study of miracles, and unearthed the password

to my maternal genes among the fibres of myology.
Oh happy sadness. Then I was pushed onto a crash
course in mathematics. The pages turned smudgy.

I couldn't subtract, and talked algebraic gibberish.
The end-of-term exam trapped me in a Venn diagram
of mother and child. Clasped within that squashed

heart, I floated out after dark, into the slow stream,
the unmothering class, which I came to haunt
for years, bringing laments like petals in my palm.

Until I graduated; tiptoeing, glossary in hand – a truant.

Your Hands

You're one year further away
yet I can draw you closer a moment,
reach out for your hands –

the slender fingers that purpled in winter,
once flowed over typewriter keys
making a clatter music, and flurried
among the bubbles of the twin-tub.

Your hands loved to mend
by disinfecting: a smear of Germolene
followed by a sting as strong as a kiss.
You'd arrange a plaster as if setting a jewel.

Much later, when all the elements of you
were closing down,
I watched you struggling to pluck
the daisies printed on your skirt

and then your hands stilled too.
For three days your right hand lay clenched
in the hollow of your pelvis,
while your left hand fanned out on the sheet,

almost in welcome, or perhaps to clasp
your mother's hand
across the bridge of half a century.
I lifted your open hand, twined it in mine,

and asked you to guide me
once more, before I was on my own.

Breakfast With My Brother

Being with you sends me mathematical.
Once every three months for two hours:
you are the measurer and I don't ask for more.

Breakfast in our house was on the run
or not at all, so I'm dreaming butter scrolls,
little pools of jam and marmalade.
You bone your kippers with bliss.
My poached eggs taste smoke-fished.

A waiter glides across the chessboard floor
with king-size teapots and jugs of water.
I'm hushed by the vaulted ceiling,
the undertones of subtracting and telling.
Numbers are chambers, safe but chilly.

When you sketch a triangle on your paper mat –
the history of Catholicism –
I listen, because ever since I taught you
with flashcards we've relished the free fall
into words, the landing in an unknown.

You ask me to define 'elegy'
although we still call this 'brekkie'.
Lost and wandering, I try to keep one eye
on the X of the clock; the minutes are slipping,
your office just footsteps away.

Shall I say this instead of goodbye?
You used to sleep in a cot beside my bed.
Your face opened my morning.

The Secret Places of the Stairs

Our last stairs were my mother's nightmare.
What if her arms gave way and she dropped the baby?

       I'm taking lessons on how to lift him.
       A little river runs down the back of his skull,
       he has frog's legs and no words.

       We are a plain family but he
            is our sparkle   through the dark.

         *

                 Mother's bungalow.

                 We can't run away
            from the troubles and cares:

              there's no space between
         day and night loving and hating

            no disappearing   into quiet.
         Ghosts smoke down a stair shaft.

              Euphemisms blossom.
       Hundreds of muscles die silent deaths.

           Frozen on the half-landing
      of every morning, that unforgiving curve.

    How to keep a foothold. Such a long way still
                     to the floor.

              Small wheels squeak
       as they plough furrows in carpets.

              Shoes last for decades.

I am always escaping skywards to learning.

No wonder I grow short-sighted,
one hand capturing
                                        star-words
the other rummaging
                        through clouds
        for buried stories.

I never look behind, but remember
        the clefts where I could shelter –
                                        so much further to fall now
I might crash-land   shattering bones.

The danger of getting above myself.

*

        Marks and Spencer staircase of my big disobedience –
                I'm falling
                        into
                        myself.
                The longest
                journey.

        I come round on an upper floor where no customers go.
                A doctor smiles at the roses
        on my dress while he sews up the corner of my mouth.

                Not embroidered stitches. Tar-slashes
                        like thorns.

*

Faint, I can't follow my younger brother up all five hundred and nine
                              spiral steps of Cologne Cathedral.

                              *

        My grandmother as a young woman, pulled
        up and down
                by a line of bells
                with brass labels. Blue Room. Tapestry Room.
                        Perhaps she hummed a tune as she ran
                        to a summons from above. Her dreams –

        she scrubbed them into those treads
        dragged her legs every night
                up the primitive steps to the attic
                                        not knowing
                        she would polish her way
                        down enough stairs in a lifetime

                        to reach heaven early   at the age of forty-two.

                              *

Running up and down three flights
keeps me in fine fettle, people say.
                        On the upper floor I am stilled –
                        writing letters, following the moon –
but I belong downstairs too
with the blacklead and beeswax.

                              *

Where *are* you?
He leaves an ascending scale of messages.
I know he dreads I've fallen
                    down those stone stairs we love and fear.

For a moment I see myself, his wife,
        spine wrought to an S.
                Over the border   he can't gather my hollow bones
                from where I winged upwards   to the light.

                            *

Does he know I have more staircases than I could ever hold together?

Autosomal Recessive Inheritance

I am the unaffected carrier of one faulty gene.
Though it's proved harmless enough on its own,

it can't transmit the intricate message,
in the right order, for my cells to read. Recessive.

I sense this hidden gene, sapped and broken.
But the working copy on the partner chromosome,

from my father, knows its task, sends
the correct instructions to the muscles, each cell:

how to create the critical protein, *Calpain 3*.
My back-up copy toils, keeps the dystrophy at bay.

Sometimes, when running up the stairs, I thank
my body's largest muscle, the gluteus maximus,

for extending power to my thigh and hip;
the gift of fluent footsteps, of worn-out slippers.

Sometimes I imagine the gene as a chain
of letters that wheelchaired a woman away –

was its sequence disrupted, a codon inserted
or deleted, the recipe too long or too short?

Sometimes I let myself remember the girl
carrying those two faulty copies, her turmoil

as she tried to cycle, or climb a slope. My mother,
unlucky with the laws of chance, the one in four.

My Mother's Salt Coat

It was no longer possible for her to glance
over her shoulder; there was grinding forward only.
The lining gritted her skin.

But the salt coat kept her upright,
sheltered her from windlash. Her back ached,
as if she was carrying all her grandmothers.

She'd imagine dropping handfuls of berries
into the pockets – then they'd burst,
shedding redness down the coat,

the stain turning the road ahead of her
the same colour the world was
from behind closed eyelids.

At dusk the coat crust was a snow-blue white,
icing her for the winter.
Yet she had disobeyed no one.

The buttons were salt crystals still growing;
at night they glinted
until thieves followed her

and she almost longed to be robbed of this greatcoat.
The taste of it thirsted her out,
the swallowing and swallowing

as lost dogs licked her into a pillar.
Her pulse stuttered, the silence soft –
she was locked inside the monument of her body.

Self-Portrait in Watercolour

First I stroked in two hundred and six bones,
waited for the raw sienna to speckle.

The hand I brushed on was watery, restless,
and when I scraped a layer of umber
from my pelvis, it moaned.

I spiralled an iris of cobalt blues
round my pupil – such joy, until that eye
encircled me and I couldn't blot it out

so it was some time before I tackled my brain.
I shushed it with a sponge.

I splashed my heart in stalwart red,
smudged out the streaks
to reveal the white highlights of arteries.

Last of all I spilled little pools
of ultramarine and alizarin crimson
and let them flood together before morning.

There, in place of an ovary, a bloom grew.
I touched it softly – was it a bruise,

or a daughter, asleep in her aumbry?

Motherland

The baby is no more than a cobweb.
It brushes off as I flurry past,
no smooth passage through.

I keep going away, I keep coming back
to dryness, the other side of tears.
Even in famines, babies are born.

No one would hear if I sorrowed
yet I'm not so far from the women
who blanket-wrap their child, a gift.

I stamp my frozen feet
towards empty shelves;

ice myself in and wait.
Snowdrifts blur my body.

I'm hungry enough for two.

For a Daughter

My name would not be your middle name.

You wouldn't inherit my listomania, I promise:
I'd renounce list-making in honour of your birth.

The term Muscular Dystrophy would not be sewn into you.

I would not pass on my stony ova
or the euphemisms stuffed up the sleeve like handkerchiefs.

Thank You wouldn't be your mantra; it trapped me at the amber light.

You wouldn't stare at every dog and see only its bite.

You would never know that *worry* derives from *wyrgan*, to strangle:
I'd lock the door to my mother's worrymongery,

but I would be your guide in the storehouse of the thesaurus,
assure you there's no such curse as being too clever.

I'd show you how to blow a trumpet in a long and steady tone.

My desk and my blue propelling pencil would be yours.

I'd hand you your great-grandmother's last letter to her daughter
from the hospital – *bye bye, dear*

All my words would be yours, so you'd observe me on the page,
all that I am and was and should have been.

And, my daughter, each night I'd hum you a lullaby.
You would remember me as song, not apology.

Never so much as larva

This miniature raincoat in *Stop!* red,
black spots on cuffs and collar,
the giant ladybird pocket –
I see her running through puddles,
mud-spatter on her bare legs;
I hear her shapeless coat squeak
with every jump and swoop.
Now she's huddled on the doorstep,
straining to steady her hand
as she paints dot after dot
onto red wellington boots.
Her brilliance from such a distance
stuns me. And as I reach out
my finger to touch this happy coat
on its peg, I almost laugh but
it still makes no sense that I miss
the daughter who was never
so much as larva or egg within me,
and all I can do at this moment
is bolt home to write her alive.

Go gentle

and all thy life be happiness and love
Note left by a mother with her child at The Foundling Hospital

I nested my daughter in a little basket,
  with three tokens to speak for me:
    an acorn, a violet, an egg-shaped pearl.

I read my daughter a story, to lull her to sleep
  for ever: the polar bear whose bath taps
    were *cold* and *icy*. She wanted more, more.

I spilled my daughter a droplet at a time
  in secret. A shame-trail of spots, her footprints.
    She was outside me, and still inside.

I pencilled my daughter into my notebook,
  prayed she would fade. She reappeared
    in my diary; I couldn't not remember.

I tucked my daughter up in one of my dreams,
  somewhere between midnight and dawn,
    so I'd be free in the daylight.

I entrusted my daughter to the castle
  where a green lady with a bundle in her arms
    drifts past the clock tower, to the cliffs.

I surrendered my daughter at the border
  of the debatable land. For years, over and over.
    She was a sunset, a cathedral of colours.

Every time I dropped my daughter like a foundling,
  I ran back to reclaim her,
    to bring her home. Her soft name.

After Green

One summer not so far from here,
when all the botanists had lost
their leafy voices, when mothers
had dulled and withered

into an endangered species, crackling
through the dust-walled valleys
because their sons had flooded
into the river and escaped like an army

of petals on the raft of its back,
when dreams turned grassy,
when fear had run dry,
there grew a longing, a thirst,

to drift away as only the newborn can,
to be lowered into a basket
and willowed slowly asleep.

The Twins' Heads

Three pounds at birth, the twins were laid in a drawer,
thought unlikely to survive. Their mother poured

all the warmth from June to August into her sons.
Their skin was thin, their skulls almost unborn;

cotton caps swamped their not-quite-arrived eyes.
Hats padded with tissue, the twins looked so surprised

their sister, ten years older, resolved to learn to knit.
From a simple pattern she made eggshell blue bonnets

for the brothers she hadn't wanted – one, let alone
two. Plain garter stitch: cast on, knit, cast off; she wove

and looped them slowly into her life, as if her hands
were willing their bones to grow. Measuring their heads,

she traced the gaps and seams that mustn't be pressed.
Their faces were double, twice as defenceless.

Monozygotic. No-one understood then that the embryo,
just two cells big, had split perfectly in two.

For years only their mother and their sister knew
which boy was which, though could never explain how.

And even now as the twins turn seventy-six,
their heads cold again, they share matching quirks –

nervous cough of a laugh, diluted eyes, the silence
followed by slipping over words mid sentence –

and each time they black out, another thread snaps
or a knot tightens. They can no longer be wrapped

up, holes darned, by the arthritic fingers of a sister
who's glitter-sharp. But she can't fathom the mystery

of what goes on in the twins' heads any more;
far away as when they were side by side in the drawer.

The Madonna of the Well
Santa Maria in Via, Rome

Just as this painting of Mary
rose to the surface of a well
that overflowed in the Cardinal's stable
one night seven and a half centuries ago,
horses panicking, the grooms running
to marvel at the slate
floating light as a canvas above the rim
yet unable to grasp it;
just as the Cardinal arrived,
swathed himself in his robes and prayed,
then waded through the flood
and rescued the image, held it to his chest,
whereupon the waters receded;
just as the Madonna was granted an altar,
the stable converted to a shrine,
and embedded in the new church;

so, today, there are still miracles,
simple and small:
worshippers, learners, even sceptics
come to drink from the well;
almost pulsing through, they pause
below Mary's subdued blue and gold;
the good mothers glow
among the flawed and sorrowing mothers,
the great-great-grandmothers wander,
the fresh-as-bread children drift
with the stone children, all
drawing from this side chapel
set deeper than the others,
where I sense, here too,
is the silent tread,
the breath, of my child.

Our Letters

I spent days learning the shorthand of your script,
wondered if you'd set me a test,
if you feared being deciphered by me.

My letters to you, too neat to remain private.
Twenty-five years later the bundles have merged,
and lie deep in our wardrobe.

These pages are evidence of our breath.
Neither son nor daughter, not even a niece
to pass them on to, I realise now.

When we're too old for journeys in the world,
will we step through our letters once more,
order them into the conversation they were?

But one of us must be left behind.
Will you or I sleep with writing below
the pillow? Or drop an envelope by the door,

so morning brings a message of welcome,
the almost touching of fingertips
not very far from a brush of the lips.

Notes

p 3   Two Gardens
Claire Goll (1891-1977), a German writer and journalist, had a love affair
and a written correspondence with Rilke. She and her second husband, the
poet Ivan Goll, were close to the Surrealist movement in literature; both
wrote in French and German.

pp 5-6   The Siege Swallow and Homing
Olga Berggolts (1910-75) lived through the 900-day Siege of Leningrad,
during which she broadcast her poems and other works on Radio Leningrad.
Both poems are versions of translations from the original Russian by Daniel
Weissbort ('Twentieth Century Russian Poetry', ed John Glad and Daniel
Weissbort, University of Iowa Press, 1992).

p 16   How much has been postponed
Vergangenheitsbewältigung – German noun meaning 'overcoming the past'.

p 18   I told no one
to rummle – to search through
to flichter – to rush about excitedly
to ba – to hush (a child) to sleep

p 30   A Splinter
plait school – a rural school where small children worked long hours learning
and practising the craft of straw plaiting for minimal pay.

p 31   Thrashing the Holy Linens
Description of the drowning drawn from the Hull Daily Mail, November 24th
1890.

p 37   Spinning Cobwebs
proving – a custom in many rural areas whereby a woman would only marry
once she was pregnant, thus having proved her fertility.

p 40   Red-ochreing Doorsteps
Only one official reference to Ann Hollingsworth exists, in the 1881 census.

p 42   Running Along the Furrows of Shirts
bundling – a rural betrothal custom when a couple slept together fully clothed.
The last apparent trace of Sarah Elizabeth Wright is in the 1901 census.

p 64   The Secret Places of the Stairs
Title from The Song of Solomon, Chapter 2, King James Bible.

p 68   Autosomal Recessive Inheritance
Humans have 46 chromosomes – 22 pairs (the autosomes) and two sex chromosomes. Genes on the autosomes are present in two copies – one on each of the two chromosomes in a pair. If one of these gene copies is faulty and the other normal gene copy compensates, the faulty gene is termed recessive and is harmless. Recessive genes only have an effect if a person has two faulty copies. Most people carry several autosomal recessive faulty genes without knowing it, but two unrelated people rarely carry the same faulty gene. Related people, however, may carry the *same* faulty gene. If two parents are related and both carry the same faulty gene, then each of their children has a one in four chance of inheriting both faulty genes and of being affected by a hereditary condition.

p 74   Go gentle
Dropped became the accepted term for the mothers who brought their children into the Foundling Hospital and left them in the hospital's care.

Praise for Anne Ryland's first collection, *Autumnologist*:

"Above all, Ryland's verse is so mesmeric that I want to keep quoting it. She is, too, an accomplished poet artlessly switching voice, line length, form ... this is the best collection I've read in a long while ..."

   –   Gail Ashton, *Envoi*

"Ryland's subtle, finely wrought poems repay however much attention the reader brings to bear upon them."

   –   Paul Batchelor, *Acknowledged Land*

"Ryland's is a poetry of awe at the world's mystery ..."

   –   Belinda Cooke, *Acumen*